MW01413339

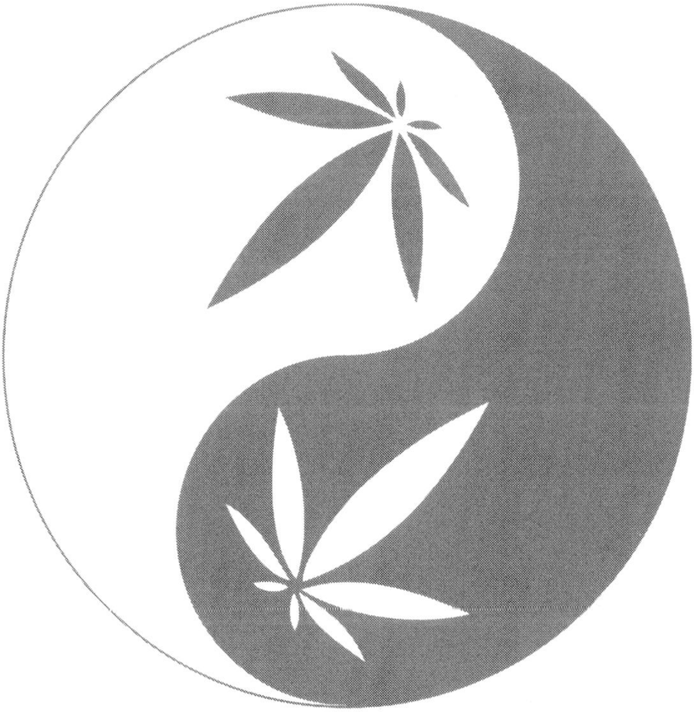

First Edition - Paperback
© 2013 Way Of Infinite Harmony
www.WayOfInfiniteHarmony.org
ISBN 978-1-291-46095-7

All rights reserved. No part of this book may be reproduced or transmitted in any form or by any means, electronic or mechanical, including photocopying, recording, or by any information storage and retrieval system without the written permission of the author, except where permitted by law.

You may ask yourself, "Who is The Green Goddess?"
The Green Goddess is a Bodhisattva.
She is the divine feminine spirit that lives within the Cannabis plant.
She is the Goddess of Liberation and Delight.
She has a gentle but powerful voice for the suffering.
She has given Her gift of the sacred Cannabis plant to the world.
The Green Goddess shares with us the therapeutic and holistic powers of the Cannabis plant.
Her gifts are magical and healing. They include beautiful fabrics, the highest quality paper and essential oils.
She is a compassionate caregiver who asks for mercy, freedom and justice for all who need Her.
The Green Goddess mourns, for those who in passing have been incarcerated for Her cause.
She prays for the veils of ignorance to be lifted from the eyes of the masses.

Legend of the Green Goddess

Way of Infinite Harmony

Path of Her Holiness Princess Ma Gu, Goddess of Cannabis

Ma Guāng Wéi

麻光为

Table of Contents

Introduction *1*
What is the Way of Infinite Harmony? *2*
Who is Ma Gu? *3*
Beliefs and Practices *5*

Teachings of The Way of Infinite Harmony *7*

Ma Gu Xian Shou *11*
The Scripture of Infinite Harmony *15*
Ma Gu, The Princess of Cannabis Her Generation and Mission *17*
Ma Gu's Pond *23*
When The World Was Green *25*
There was a Goddess Named Ma Gu *31*
The Seduction and Abduction *33*
Ripples Sifting Sand *39*
Wang Yuan and Ma Gu *41*
Traditional Oral Teachings *49*

Puja and Cannabis Meditation: *53*

Puja *55*
Meditation *59*

Pilgrimage and Festivals: *63*

Ma Gu Temple *65*
Ma Gu Wonderland *66*
The Ma Gu Mountains *67*
Festivals & Important Dates *69*

Appendix: 75

Different Accounts: 77
  Arrayed Marvels 77
  Garden of Marvels 77
  Commoner of Fuyang 78

Introduction

This book contains the complete written Teachings of The Way of Infinite Harmony. A selection of Oral Teachings. Explanations of the practices and beliefs of devotees. Cannabis Meditation guidance, and details of sacred sites and festival dates connected to Her Holiness Princess Ma Gu, Goddess of Cannabis.

Many of the texts have never been published in English before and are available here for the first time.

What is the Way of Infinite Harmony?

The Way of Infinite Harmony is a Taoist sect based on the Immortalization of Her Holiness Princess Ma Gu, Goddess of Cannabis.

The aim of followers of Ma Gu is to attain the Tao (the Ultimate, the One, the All-That-Is). It is not to corrupt people and force them to take "drugs". Devotees believe the individual should decide whether to use Cannabis or not.

However, devotees do believe that Cannabis is the key to understanding the Self and attaining true internal cultivation, as shown to us by Her Holiness.

The Way of Infinite Harmony is not a Church or Temple based group, Ma Gu Temple has never been an institution but rather a sacred and holy place.

Who is Ma Gu?

Ma Gu is the Taoist Goddess of Cannabis.

Her full name and title is Her Holiness Princess Ma Gu, Goddess of Cannabis.

Other names often heard include; Ma Gu, Ma Ku, Maid Ma, Cannabis Lady, Princess of Cannabis, Hemp Lady, Cannabis Goddess, Hemp Goddess, Green Goddess, Mother Cannabis, Cannabis Maid, Hemp Maid, Cannabis Maiden & Hemp Maiden.

Ma Gu is often depicted flying on a crane, riding a deer and holding peaches or wine (symbols of longevity).

She has the forever youthful appearance of an eighteen year old girl, though her actual age is infinite.

The most famous of all the stories that feature Ma Gu is Ma Gu Xian Shou ("Ma Gu Offers Longevity"). In the story, Ma Gu attends a peach banquet held by the Queen Mother of the West (Xi Wang Mu), for which she brews a special wine made of Cannabis.

The acceptance of the wine Ma Gu offers is seen as verification by the deities that the Path of Ma Gu (Way of Infinite Harmony) is a path to the Tao. This is because in the Taoist pantheon the Queen Mother of The West is the ancestor of Female Immortals, meaning that all women who have attained immortality in the three realms and ten directions, in Heaven or in the human world, are under the rule of the Queen Mother of the West.

In 1116 Emperor Hui Zong, Heaven's representative on Earth, gave her the title of Immortal Xu Miao (Infinite Harmony).

Devotees use the words "Ma Gu Xian Shou" as a statement of faith, and believe hearing these words gets one closer to attaining the Tao / knowing the Self. It is also therefore often said as a mantra.

Ma Gu Xian Shou

麻姑獻壽

Beliefs and Practices

The beliefs of the Way of Infinite Harmony are Taoist.

Devotees follow the example and teachings of Her Holiness Princess Ma Gu, Goddess of Cannabis (Taoist Immortal Xu Miao) as understood from the scriptures.

These teachings will be revealed to the spiritual practitioner who reads the sacred texts published within this book with an open heart.

As well as the complete set of Way of Infinite Harmony texts contained in this book, devotees recommend reading the Daozhang (Taoist Canon), primarily the Tao Te Ching, Chuang Tzu, Lieh Tzu, Hua Hu Ching and Wen Tzu.

The interpretation of these texts is up to the practitioner. Being of the lineage of the Hermit there are no strict rules to follow as regards diet, ritual, meditation etc... It is however generally accepted that if smoking Cannabis it should be pure and not mixed with tobacco.

To follow the Way of Infinite Harmony just open your heart to Ma Gu, consume the Herb of which She is co-terminus and while in this most blissful and sacred state the Gate to the Mystery of Mysteries can open.

Teachings of The Way of Infinite Harmony

The complete translated texts of the Way of Infinite Harmony, Path of Her Holiness Princess Ma Gu, Goddess of Cannabis.

麻姑献寿

麻姑獻壽

献寿图

一九八七年十二月十八日采菊客于多伦山馆

Ma Gu Xian Shou

Ma Gu is the Goddess of Cannabis. The common people would often marvel at Her beauty, and no matter when people saw Her, She was always as young as a lady of 18 or 19 years old.

According to legend, one night Ma Gu's father had a dream in which he was fishing on a river and hooked a lotus flower and the next morning his wife gave birth to a baby girl. A baby of extraordinary beauty and exceptional hearing. At three months she was able to talk, at 1 year old She was able to read poetry and at the age of seven She was able to walk on water in Her shoes.

Legend has it that Ma Gu's father was an evil man who would force his workers to toil as slaves until the roosters crowed three times. Ma Gu's heart went out to them and She petitioned Her father to give them more rest, but he refused. Then Ma Gu realized that if She could make the roosters crow the workers would finish earlier, so She would imitate a roosters call and start all the roosters crowing much earlier than normal. When Her father heard of what She had done he was furious and disowned his beautiful daughter.

Ma Gu then traveled to the mountains where She practiced Self-cultivation.

One day, Ma Gu was visited by four fairies who informed Her that the Queen Mother of the West was inviting Her to the Immortal Peach Banquet and asked what gift would She be preparing for it?

Ma Gu replied:

"I have nothing of value for her. But I shall brew some wine"

The fairies were delighted at the thought of drinking Ma Gu's wine and told Her they would see Her at the banquet.

Ma Gu set to work brewing Her wine, using only the finest top buds of Cannabis. Before long it was the date of the banquet and Ma Gu's wine was ready.

When She arrived at Kunlun Palace the four fairies excitedly rushed to Ma Gu to smell Her wine all exclaiming "It's so fragrant!"

Deities, immortals and buddhas all came to the grand peach banquet of the Queen Mother of the West. The fairies introduced Ma Gu to the Queen Mother and Ma Gu presented the wine to her:

"I offer longevity. Drinking a cup of my wine will give a long and fortunate life. I would like to wish my immortal master ten-thousand years of celebration, and to live as long as the star of the south celestial pole. By drinking this exquisite elixir, you will not get older as the years, one after another, pass by."

The Queen Mother accepted the wine and took a sip:

"Unbelievable! Wine has never tasted so good!"

The Queen Mother of the West then told Ma Gu to serve the wine to all her guests declaring:

"Ma Gu Xian Shou"

麻姑獻壽

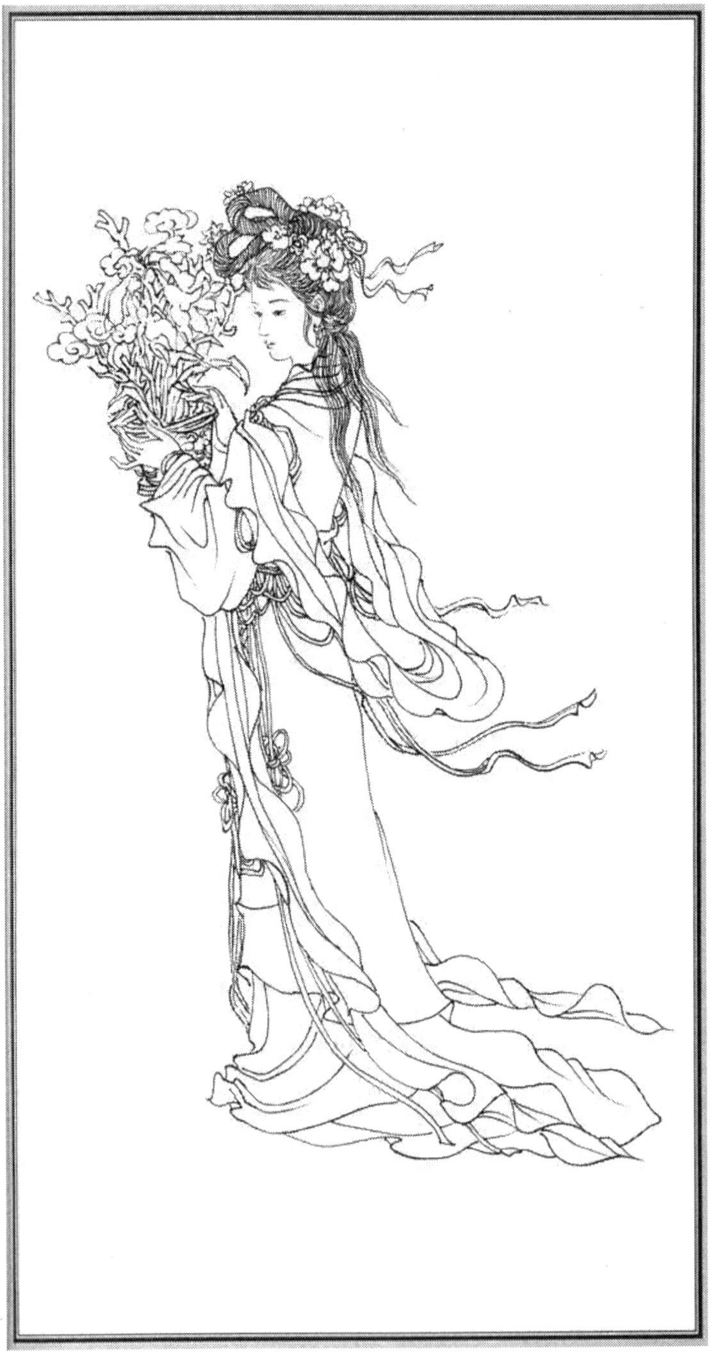

The Scripture of Infinite Harmony

The Goddess does dwell within the Plant co-terminus; One and the same Being.

The Goddess-Plant and Her transformative properties.

Upon the ingestion of the Plant as food, smoke or extracted chemical there is a mystical union with the Princess of Cannabis, Ma Gu.

In this most sacred and holy state the devotee can discover the true nature of the world and the true nature of the Self.

麻姑献寿

Ma Gu, The Princess of Cannabis
Her Generation and Mission

During the countless cycles of generation and decay within the vegetative world many mutations occurred in the grand harmony of the garden. These mutations were perfectly natural, but no one not even the All See-er within could predict how or when the mutations would occur, these were the natural spontaneous transformations of the garden's Way. One could expect nothing, but one had to be prepared for anything.

Deep within the jungle forest where hardly an animal roamed, except for the huge three legged, six armed, wise elephant-ape-man, there was a fathomless spring which formed a large pool at the base of a mountain. Many giant trees had fallen across the pool; it was a deep clear crisp blue-green pool, and in it there was a blue-green algae.

The elephant-ape-creature was the strongest and the wisest creature in the deep jungle, he had a short trunk and large powerful tusks which he used to uproot trees. The elephant-man was wise because he cleared the Way through the jungle. He removed trees and thick brush, making paths and road Ways from one location to the next in a very systematic order. If one was lost in the jungle, one had only to follow an elephant-ape-man and one could find one's Way again. He was certainly a wise and strong creature deep within the jungle.

One day the elephant-ape-man was taking his daily drink of water at this mysterious blue-green algae pool when a huge tree fell almost right on top of him cutting one of his arms. The cut started to bleed and some of the blood splashed into the pool. The three legged creature then hopped off with a mighty bound and swung through the trees with such a howl that the birds flew in every direction. As one of the large eagle-snake birds launched from its perch above the pool, one of it's feathers fell into the pool too.

The elephant-man's blood and the eagle-snake's feather created a chemical reaction within the pool and the blue-green algae began to transform becoming psychoactive; as the composition of the pool altered a belch of volcanic gas bubbled up out of the crack at the bottom of the fathomless pool. As the bubble broke the surface, sulfur fumes sprayed out along with the now reddish-blue-green algae and the surrounding vegetation withered badly. By the next day almost every plant in the area was dead. But one little seed bearing weed, now covered with dead reddish-brown algae, had somehow survived. The psychoactive properties of the algae were transmitted to its genetic structure. This little wild flower was clearly dying too, but its basic life impulse to survive was working hard to reproduce some seed in preparation for its regeneration. There was only one such wild weed flower of its kind in the region and it really needed some external pollen to fertilize itself. The son of Father Sky, the wind, observed the life and death struggle there in the heart of the jungle, and he blew some cool breezes that way to sooth the hot burnt spot around the now reddish brown pool. The breeze picked up pollen and some of his sister, the powerful creative dust. The pollen and dust alight on the sex organs of the little dying wild flower, and the receptive organs suck it in like parched soil after a light rain. Within a short time the wild flower did seed. A little tiny yellow, orange and red mouse-like humming-bird flew by and saw the purple seeds and slowed its flight to eat the seeds. It swallowed them whole.

The red, yellow and orange mouse-like humming-bird made its daily journey throughout and all around the grand green garden. At nightfall it crawled into its burrow at the base of a huge sap-oak tree that dripped a thick syrup which the little bird did love so much. Before retiring for the night the little bird filled its belly, as it usually did, with the thick syrup, and lied down to sleep. To sleep, to sleep and to dream, never to awake again. Some say the bird was old and ready to die; others say though it was old it could have lived many more years as most of its kind, and they attribute its death to the mixture of seed and syrup. Only the Fairy of Dreams knows for sure what really happened that night. Before the little bird died, it dreamed some wild and lucid dreams. Dreams filled with purple smoke clouds and a faint but growing image of a glowing form taking shape. Within the purple clouds of its dream, there was at first chaos and disorder; the clouds reeled and spun forming a vortex and then a counter-vortex. And slowly in the mist and chaos a substance began to settle out, and then, it began to take on form and shape. By day break, the purple seed in the now dead bird's belly surrounded by the syrup germinated. A little while passed and soon there was a strong stalk protruding from the burrow opening, and there beside the tree lay the glowing dazzling, ever so beautiful, and fragrant Ma Gu, Princess of Cannabis. She stirred a little, rolled over and saw the huge stalk growing beside her, smiled and closed her eyes to sleep and dream again.

In Her vision She saw the plant grow and grow and grow, and as it grew every branch began to seed and seed and seed. And in Her dream, the meaning of Her Immortal life was revealed unto Her, namely, that She must plant the seed of this reddish blue-green wild-flower everywhere. It was Her calling in Immortal life, Her "Mission" A goddess, an archetype, was born this morn. A true unselfish gift of the family of Sky and Earth, sun and wind, dust, water and plant was presented to the world this morn. Cannabis was born. A good strong hardy weedy flower, fine for making rope and thatch, but a plant also endowed with divine quality. The Goddess does dwell within the plant co-terminus; one and the same being, the Goddess-Plant and her transformative properties. Upon the ingestion of the plant as food, smoke, or extracted chemical analysis, there is a mystical union with the Princess of Cannabis, Ma Gu, and in this most sacred and holy state of rapture and ecstasy, the devotee can also discover the true nature of the world and the true nature of the Self, that all is impermanent, that there is only continuity among the interrelationships of the parts.

So when Ma Gu, the Princess of Cannabis, awoke, the stalk was some fifteen feet high, with five main branches, at every leaf stem there were five lateral shoots, and each and every bud was loaded with seed. Ma Gu rolled out Her cape under the huge tree and shook its stalk, and the seed covered her cape which she rolled up. Being daughter of weed and bird, dust and wind, and an Immortal in her own right with all the magical powers that come with Immortality, Ma Gu flew off into the Sky. Almost instinctively she flew the route of the little yellow, red and orange mouse-like humming bird with the seed. She flew all around and throughout the grand green garden, while She flew She slowly unrolled Her cape and the seed fell to Earth, and it fell and it fell and it fell all over the place. When She flew past the burnt now reddish-brown blue-green pool, She felt a faint glimmer of nostalgia and home sickness. So She landed there to walk about and to gently stroke a dead withered flower. She also lay many a seed in that region. Within a short while all the seed was planted about Earth, and by nightfall almost every one was germinating.

By the turning of noon the day after next the garden was full of the fragrance of Ma Gu, and almost everywhere there She was manifested in the particular plants, reddish-brown blue-green flower buds oozing a thick syrup-like resin loaded with mystical powers of insight. All the animals ate freely of this plant, smiled, took a nap and dreamt of the true nature of the world and the true nature of the Self.

麻姑獻壽

Ma Gu's Pond

Green plains of lush fields,
Green rolling foot hills,
Green, deep blue green mountains.
Far up the Eastern trail,
The Temple of Lao Tzu.
On the side,
Green Pond of Ma Gu.

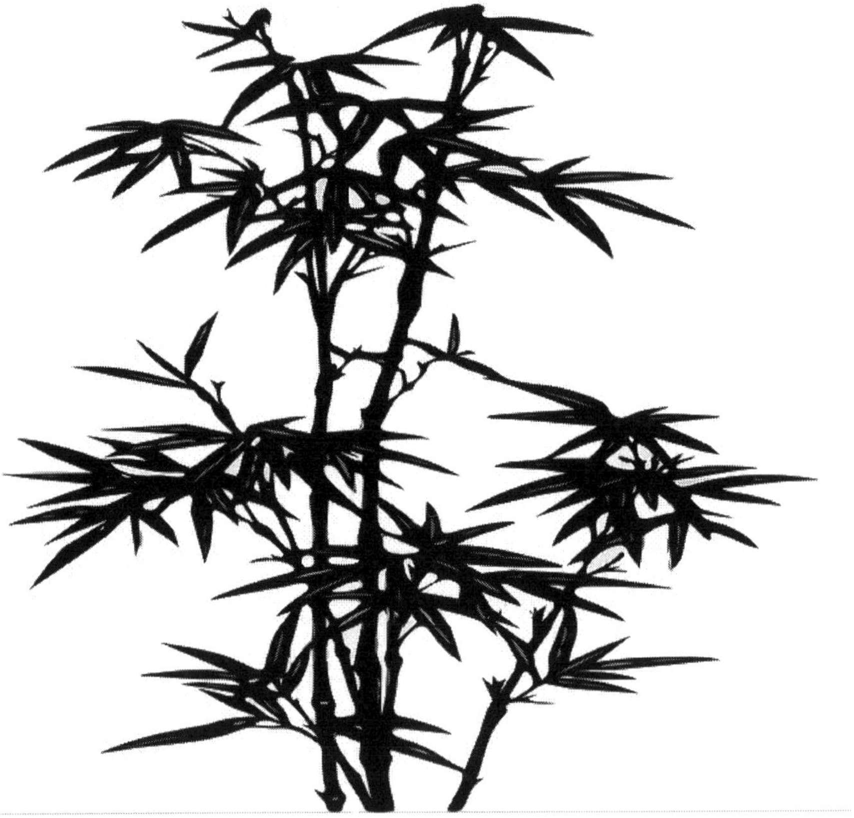

When The World Was Green

A long, long, long time ago, some used to say "in the Beginning" but now we know better, back in one of the infinite beginning-less and endless cycles of cosmic generation and decay, the world was covered in various shades of green vegetation. The world was a grand garden. Father Sky and Mother Earth nourished the bugs, plants and animals in the garden as their children; they gave life, cultivated, pruned and harvested the plants according to the seasons and cycles of the sun and moon. The animals were allowed to run wild, eating the plants as they pleased; there was always more than enough for everyone. On occasion the animals even ate another, though rarely of their own kind.

Life and death, and even some killing, were accepted as natural. Sky and Earth gave the plants and animals life, but they did not lord it over them. They possessed the world but they did not force their presence or their desires. All was in one grand harmony; an organismic harmony where each bug and each blade of grass, every leaf on each plant contributes to the processes of the field.

One day Sky and Earth made special note of one of their children playing in the garden. They observed this creature's games and, like themselves harvesting plants and fruits from the garden, they noticed that at times both the male and the female of the species appeared not to play, but to do some work.

In particular Sky and Earth noticed that this creature preferred to eat its fruit fresh off the trees, but favored to take the nuts and seeds home to eat at leisure while laying around. The females not only nursed their young, but they also took some milk from the goats and cows and made odd but delicious things. Regrettably it was this creature who most often supplemented its diet with other animal flesh. This creature was also noted for seeking out a certain rare herb in the garden, drying it and making a fire to burn this treasured herb. Both males and females of the species together would pass a small fire of burning herb from one to another, apparently inhaling the smoke.

When this creature had found a particularly large stash of herb growing in gardens along the banks of the mountain rivers, where the sun shone bright and the water was pure, they gathered a large amount of the herb and took it out into a clearing in a pasture. They marked off a section of the ground and cleared out the grass. Then they dug a pit at one end of the rectangular area. The power woman and healer man blessed the area and a fire was begun in the pit. Father Sky and Mother Earth were intrigued by the work of the these homely creatures; they made special note of the activities. When the fire was good and hot, Sky and Earth saw their children continue to lay bundles of the top buds from their day's harvest on the fire and as the smoke began to rise from the fire pit, Sky and Earth were drawn, out of curiosity, to observe the rising columns of smoke. Soon they were soaring in the smoke, rising in its purple clouds.

Then, an insight awoke within the cosmic spirits; and they gained the wisdom of the All-Knower who dwells within. Out of the smoke a light from the fire beamed them to higher transformations of consciousness, higher than they had ever imagined, and amid the mist of the smoke and the visions they had a piercing flash of insight through which they discovered the true nature of the world and the true nature of the Self. They knew, then, that the infinite qualities of the infinite beings of the beginning-less and endless cycles of the infinite multiverses all interrelated in their particularity were totally impermanent; all was and is changing, even their own nature was one of transformation.

Heaven and Earth saw that the herb was good.

Through the purple cloud also emerged one of their lost children Ma Gu, the Princess of Cannabis, and now the family was united, the lost daughter returned home. In celebration they planted Cannabis everywhere throughout the garden; and the animals were content. The working creatures were especially happy about this, and so they performed the fire ritual in honor of Ma Gu, Sky and Earth until they were exhausted, and yet the Cannabis could be used over and over again without exhausting even the fine top buds. The world was green and the bud did flourish upon Mother Earth, and its smoke filled the void of Father Sky.

One day a group of the workers who were noted for not working very much but spending a lot of time lying and laying in the mud with the thick skinned hippopotamus and pigs. This group of worker creatures was nicknamed "the Pigs" because they did lay in the mud with the pig. Well, one day "the Pigs" got it into their wild heads that they could monopolize the bud, and so early before day break; "the Pigs" began to pick the bud, and even the leaf, even the most young saplings and seedlings; planning to store it away in a cave and exchange it for food, favors, and information about mud pits were pigs lay. By mid-morning they had done quite a bit of damage in the garden. Finally Ma Gu saw what their selfish intentions were, but She admired their new found diligence to accomplish something in life. So She smiled mercifully upon them, for every plant they picked She made two more grow. With twice as many plants in the garden it was very fragrant and potent and there was more than enough bud for everyone and many numerous fire rituals were offered in honor of this new found prosperity. "The Pigs" were so single minded in their task to harvest the massive amount of bud, that they forgot about storing it properly, they even forgot about selling it for personal profit. Most passers-by thought that "the Pigs" were finally working on behalf of the fire ritual, and so they would carry away the bundles to the cleared sacred areas in the pastures.

As space and time changed the garden too changed. In some places the garden was killed off and turned to dry desert sands. In other places the garden was sealed off from the outside world (the lost garden, and Shangrila) in other places the garden was moved inside the earth, the mountain, the home, and in some practices the garden is moved within one's mind in meditation; or it was replanted in the clouds and dreams of the workers. "The Pigs" branched off as a species through the practice of inbreeding; and some of them gained enough insight, finally, to figure out how to monopolize on the shortage of garden bud, and it finally came to pass that they would sell the herb for profit.

Even though the children do not remember when the bud was free, or how to perform the ancient fire ritual or how to live in harmony with Sky and Earth, we are slowly starting to remember the right things, and to forget the wrong ones.

麻姑祝壽圖　丁卯春頤寫於廣州

There is a Goddess Named Ma Gu

There is a Goddess named Ma Gu.
She is very youthful and pretty.
She looks like an 18 year old girl.
But in fact, She has lived for thousands of years.
Because Ma Gu has such longevity, if one accepts an offering from
Her he will also be youthful, beautiful, healthy and alive forever.

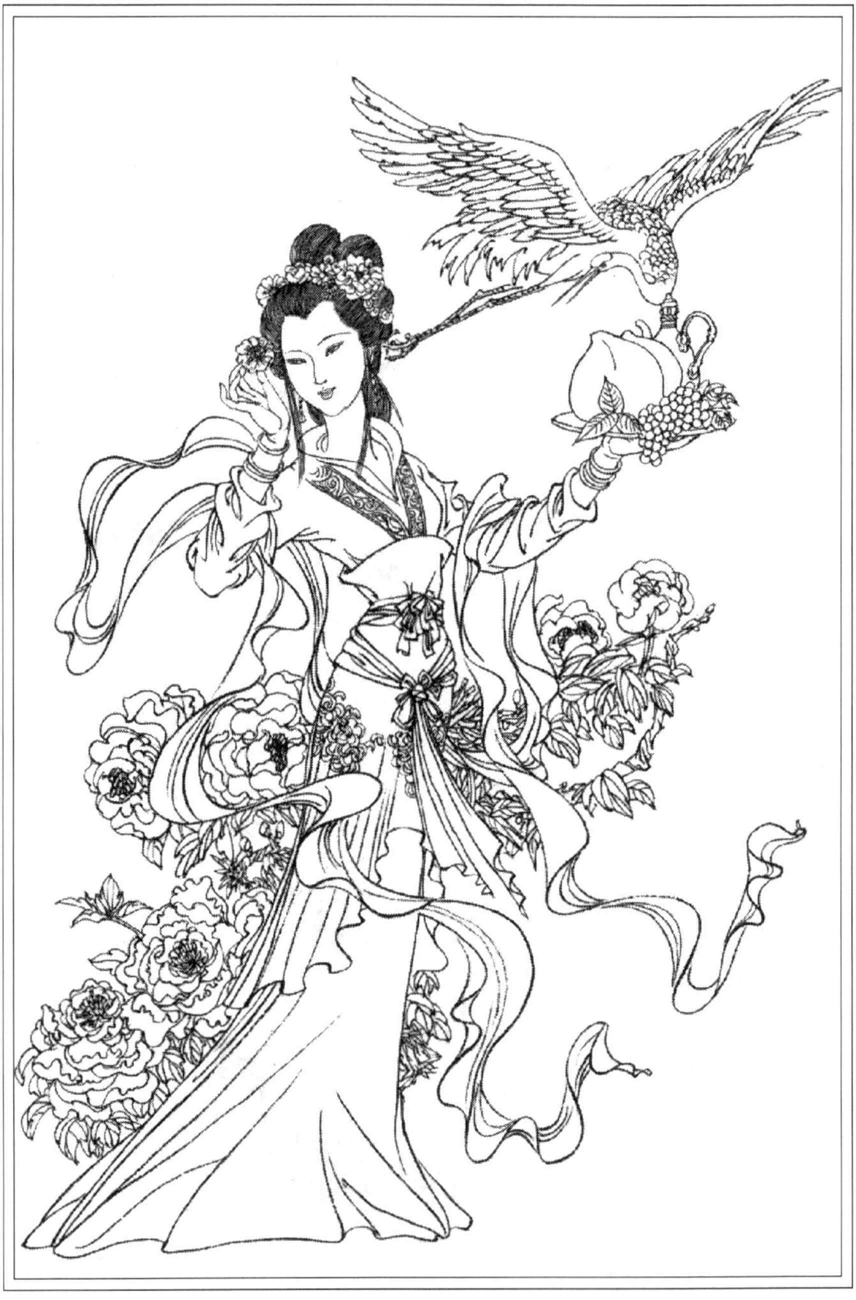

The Seduction and Abduction

One day Ma Gu was taking a stroll about the mountains and valleys which she loved best. She was day-dreaming about intimate loving and sharing contact with another for She had not yet known the enjoyment of another and was longing for some enjoyable contact. Now in this area, there lived the priest of the cosmic spirits, the god of immortality, blessing, bliss and the psilocybin mushroom, Soma the Great. Soma was always looking for a good time; he had no real desire in his immortal life but to enjoy it by bringing utter bliss to others. And so he made quite sure that his worldly manifestation, the psilocybin mushroom, did grow all about the moist regions of the grand garden; where the garden was dry he arranged for birds and other animals to import the mushroom dry.

On this day Soma did spy the lovely dazzling polychrome florescence of Ma Gu's cape and gown. There She appeared out of purple radiant clouds. She wore the lovely aspect of a fair maiden of eighteen. Her hair was partly done up in a bun, while the rest hung freely to her shapely waist and curving hips and buttock and blew about in the breeze. She was dressed in celestial cloth which radiated the colors of the rainbow. Soma just had to be with Her. But knowing that even the immortals were often put off by his massive size and dark purple color, Soma used his magical powers to transform himself into the appearance of a night fairy, a delicate creature with a light brown complexion, rosy cheeks, streaming black hair and a sensuous erotic shapely figure, and he set off down the mountain trail.

When Soma turned the bend in the trail and Ma Gu's eyes fell upon the appearance of the night fairy, she was immediately swept up in the aura of Love. In this burst of Love, Ma Gu saw a huge dark purple figure, for Love is not blind as some like to say, but Love gives one the deepest penetrating insight into the true nature of the other. The appearance of the night fairy was much more appealing to the eye. She knew, from the insight of the All-Knower-Within, that her Love was true, and that appearances are often more pleasing than reality. So She decided to play along with the appearance of the night fairy. She had been waiting for this opportunity for some time and was not about to let it slip away because of such trivialities.

The night fairy approached reciting poetic verse of greetings:

"Your most gracious welcome
Here, to my home in the wood.
Please, do with me come
My fair maiden, if you would.
I have prepared some magical wine
It comes straight off the vine.
Please, do come at my home,
There we might with the gods moan and roam".

Though Ma Gu thought the poetry was a bit strained; she deeply appreciated its sentiment and the spirit of the words; the Love connection was there, the feelings were mutual. Ma Gu went up to the night fairy, gave him a tight hug and the passionate kiss on the cheek. The fairy exchanged these favors ever so delicately, and said,

"My name is A'mos. I am a night fairy who dwells in these woods; my mission in immortal life is to fulfill dreams and bring pleasure to any and all creatures. Please, do accept my invitation to my home, and come and try some of my wine straight off the vine."

Ma Gu graciously accepted, and off they went hand in hand up the mountain trail.

Actually Soma lived and danced out in the open under sun and other stars, and only occasionally did he sit under a huge mushroom, to rest against its stalk and relax on its spongy spores. When they reached the top of the mountain, there stood a magnificent palace, gigantic towers piercing the clouds, pillars rooted in the base of the mountain, large expansive curving roofs with dropping eaves, sweet smells and fine music coming from every other corner. Ma Gu was slightly impressed, but she was much more impressed by the food, the inner heat being generated between their hands, and the tingling sensation rippling throughout her spirit-body. A'mos led them through inner chambers deep within the palace to a room which was like a microcosm. There was a magnificent fountain in the center which was fed by a hot spring at its base was a fine hot pool which emptied into a larger cooler pool. The pool was surrounded by fine delicate very soft moss and grasses, extremely delicate to the touch and very fragrant with some of the most lovely mushrooms growing all about. The rest of the room was a grand garden in its own right where the trees and bushes and rocks all provided a place to sit, recline, or lay about. There were fragrant flowers everywhere, and fruit to stimulate the five flavors. With red and purple clouds hovering about the ceiling. By the pool stood a flat rock and on it a flask of the magical wine with five glasses.

"I call this magical wine `soma'," A'mos said with a smile.

He continued,

"I always do things ritualistically. Let us sit down and perform the libation rite, and then have a little drink."

Ma Gu was impressed, but fearing that the magical wine not be strong enough for the seduction She had in mind, She imparted some of Her most potent transformative spirit into the wine, just to make sure. Of course, the wine was loaded with Soma's most potent psilocybin.

A'mos then filled the five glasses saying as He filled them: "First, one for the Tao, the Way; and then two for Sky and Earth, and one for you and one for me."

As He spoke the glass filled first appeared mysteriously to empty itself. The wine of the second glass ascended into the heavens and the third tipped over and was absorbed by Earth. After the first glass was emptied every blade of grass, every leaf, every twig, every hair and cell of every animal began to quiver. When the second goblet was emptied, the heavens let out a roar with claps of thunder and lightening, and after the third cup was emptied, Earth did quake and shake. The multiverses were quivering. Then, they toasted each other and drank freely from their bottomless goblets. Setting the drink aside they collapsed into each other's arms and entered the bliss of tantric union throughout the night. At day break they were bathing in the hot spring attempting to unravel their joined spirit-bodies. Both thought that they had surely met their soul mate.

Ma Gu did not desire to leave, but it would be impolite to stay any longer. A'mos identified her restlessness, and made the following proposal:

"Have you ever been to the islands of P'eng Lai out in the Eastern Ocean?"

"No, I have left seed there of course, but I never stopped off." Ma Gu replied.

A'mos continued:

"Since we have become lovers, I would like to offer to establish this very palace for you on the islands of P'eng Lai."

Ma Gu thought that this was a rather extravagant gift for a night fairy to be making, and so realized that Soma was revealing himself and offering his friendship.

"Well I would not want to cause you any trouble, but if you insist on making such a gift for me, it would be impolite for me to decline."

Soma replied:

"So let it be done, we begin to move to Peng Lai."

Ma Gu said:

"Then, in honor of your gift let us send out word that there will be a grand party at the new palace on Peng Lai; let us invite all the cosmic spirits, immortals, gods, and creatures; we will have a party of one-thousand years to makes sure everyone has enough time to come at least once."

When the palace appeared on the islands of Peng Lai, it was twenty times the original size, and twenty times more comfortable, and enjoyable; it could now house their guests for the thousand year party. So many immortals attended the party and stayed on afterwards that Peng Lai soon became known as the Isle of the Immortals.

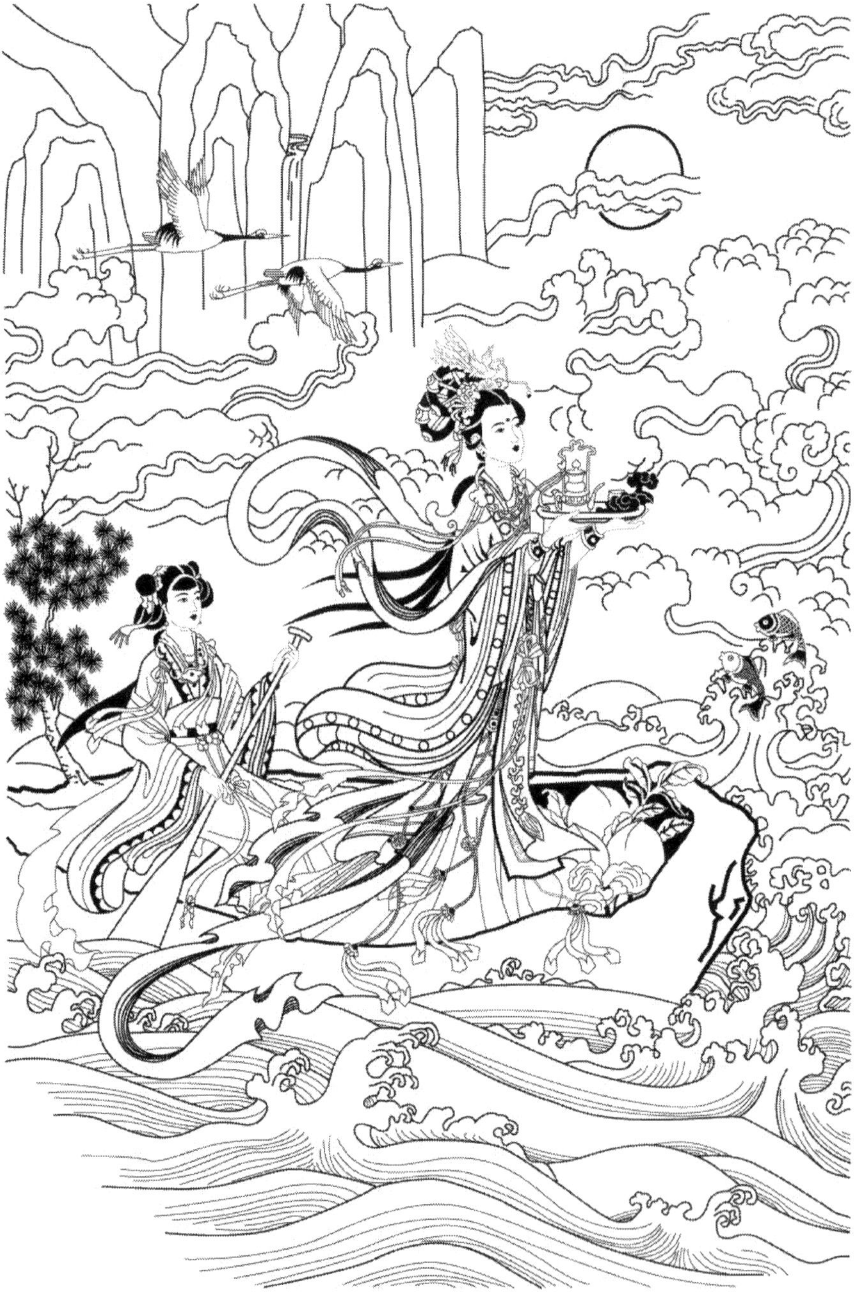

Ripples Sifting Sand

Mirage is obscure.
Ride the waves and shout in amazement,
Ignore the fools who ladle the ocean
And laugh at rivers and lakes.
Having a shower of sunshine
And bathing in the moonlight,
I will take a boat.

Can I catch six turtles?
My fishing rod touches the coral.
Ask Goddess Ma Gu about fertile fields,
And waters clear and shallow.
Misty air floats up to the sky,
The sky reaches the water.
Where is Peng Lai?

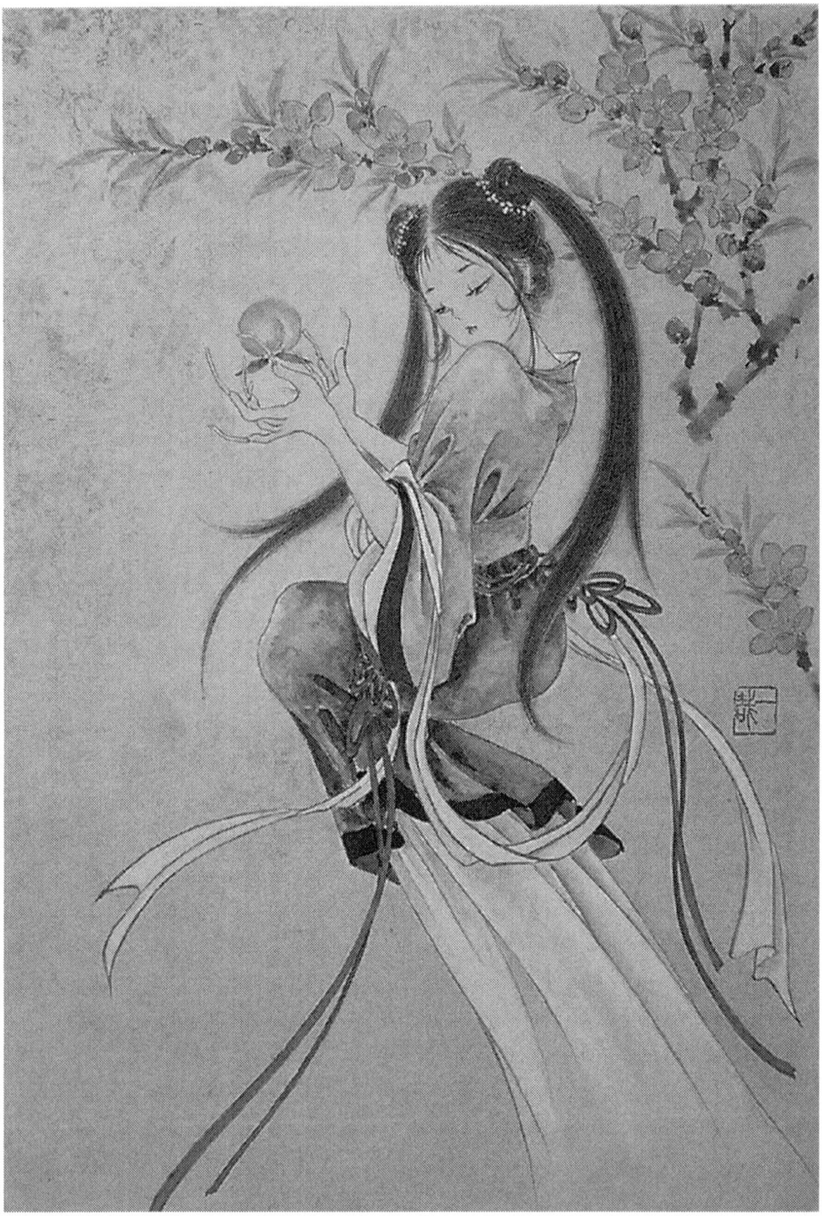

Wang Yuan and Ma Gu

Wang Yuan, styled Fanping, was a native of Donghai. He was nominated as a Filial and Incorrupt and was appointed a Gentleman of the Interior and Grand Master of Palace Leisure at Court. He broadly studied and mastered the Six Classics, but had an especially good understanding of celestial patterns and the essentials of the He and Luo River Charts and other prognosticatory weft texts. He could predict the flourishing and decline of all beings in the heavens and among men, and could foretell fortune and misfortune in the nine provinces as easily as if they were on his palm. Later he quit his offices and entered the mountains to cultivate the Tao, and by the time his Way had been completed Han Emperor Huan heard of him. The emperor summoned him to court repeatedly, but Wang would not appear. So an order was sent out to all kingdoms and commanderies to compel him to come to court. (After being brought in) Wang simply lowered his head, kept his mouth shut, and did not reply to the edict. He only wrote an inscription on the palace gate: it consisted of over four hundred words all concerning future events. The emperor disliked this and ordered the words effaced. The words on the outside (of the gate) were removed successfully, but the ones on the inside appeared even darker and were pressed into the grain of the wood. The more they were erased the more clearly they showed up.

Wang Yuan returned to his native village.

Wang Yuan had no children, the people of his village, over several generations, helped to support him with donations. A native of the same commandery, the Defender-in-Chief Chen Dan, built a Tao chamber for Wang, and morning and night he went to pay his respects to him, asking only for his blessing and saying nothing of studying the Way. Wang Yuan stayed at Chen Dan's house for over thirty years, and during all that time there was no one in Chen's family who grew sick or died, including the servants: the domestic animals flourished, and the fields and the orchards produced abundant yields.

Suddenly Wang Yuan announced to Chen Dan:

"The time has come for me to depart. I cannot remain here much longer. I will set out tomorrow at noon."

At that very hour Wang died. Chen knew he had departed as a Transcendent and so did not dare bury his body in the ground. He only wept, sighed and said

"The Master has abandoned me! How can I bear it?"

And so he prepared a coffin and funerary implements and burned incense, and he approached the bed to wrap the body in clothing. But on the third night the body disappeared: yet the cap and garments were completely undisturbed, like a cicada shell.

A little over a hundred days after Wang Yuan died. Chen Dan died, too. Some said he had obtained Wang's Way and so (merely) transformed and departed: but others say Wang knew Chen was destined to die soon, so he abandoned him and departed.

After leaving his mortal body Wang Yuan's first thought was to head east to Mount Guacang *(located in southeastern Xianju district, Zhejiang Province)*. Passing through Wu, he came to the house of Cai Jing at the Xu Gate. Cai Jing was only a peasant, but his bones and physiognomy indicated that he was fit for (eventual) transcendence. Wang Yuan realized this, and that is why he went to his home.

Said Wang to Cai:

"By birth, you are destined to transcend the world: you will be chosen as a replacement for an office. But your knowledge of the Tao is scant; you cannot ascend (directly) in this condition."

Then Wang declared to Cai the essential teachings, and left him. Soon Cai felt his entire body grow hot as if on fire. He craved cold water to bathe himself in; his entire family brought water and poured it over him, and it was like making steam by pouring water over hot rocks. This went on for three days. Then, he stood up, went into his room, and covered himself with a blanket, and vanished, only his outer skin was left, intact from head to foot, like a cicada shell.

After he had been gone more than a decade, he suddenly returned home one day. His face was that of a youth once more, and he had regained his strength: his hair had reverted to black. He announced to his family:

"Lord Wang will arrive on the seventh day of the seventh moon. On that day you must prepare great quantities of food and drink to offer his attendants."

On the appointed day, the Cai family borrowed vessels and prepared a vast quantity of beverages and food dishes, setting them out in the courtyard. Lord Wang did indeed arrive on that day. In advance of his arrival, the sound of metal drums, pipes, men and horses could be heard. The closer the sounds came, the more alarmed were the bystanders, for no-one could tell where the sounds were coming from. Then, when the party arrived at Cai's house, his entire family saw Wang. He was wearing a long journey outer coat and a crimson robe with a tiger-head belt bag, a five coloured sash, and a sword. He had a short yellow beard and was of medium stature. He was riding a feather-canopied chariot drawn by a team of five dragons, each of them a different colour. To the front and rear, the banners, pennants, insignias, and the train of armed attendants were all familiar to those of a great general when he rides out. There were five hundred soldiers in twelve ranks, their mouths all sealed with honey, all astride dragon mounts; they descended from the sky to the music of pipes and drums and hovered in midair over the courtyard. The attendants were all over ten feet high, and they did not walk as humans do.

When the entire train had arrived, all of the attendants suddenly vanished and only Wang Yuan remained visible, seated. Cai Jing's parents, siblings, and in-laws were brought and introduced. Then Wang dispatched someone to summon Ma Gu. None (of Cai's family) knew who this Ma Gu was. The summons read:

"Wang Fangping respectfully says: "It has been a long time since you were in the human realm. I have come to this place today and was wondering whether Her Holiness Princess Ma Gu, Goddess of Cannabis would like to come and converse for a while."

In a moment came a note in reply; the messenger was invisible, but the words of the note were read aloud, and they were these:

"Ma Gu bows and says: "Without our realizing it, more than five hundred years have passed since our last meeting. I am troubling your messenger to carry this to you for the moment, and I myself will arrive in the space of a meal. I must first carry out an order to stop by Peng Lai: I shall not be gone long, and as soon as I return I shall come to greet you personally. Pray do not leave until I have come."

Four hours later, Ma Gu arrived. In Her case, also the sounds of men and horses were first heard. When she arrived at Cai's home, his whole family saw Her as well.

She appeared to be a beautiful woman of eighteen or nineteen: Her hair was done up, and several loose strands hung down Her waist. Her gown had a pattern of colours, but it was not woven; it shimmered, dazzling the eyes, and was indescribable, it was not of this world. She approached and bowed to Wang, who bade Her rise. When they were both seated, they called for the traveling canteen. The servings were piled up on gold platters and in jade cups without limit. There were delicacies, many of them made from flowers and fruits, and there fragrance permeated the air inside (Cai's home) and out.

Ma Gu declared:

"Since I attained Immortality, I have seen the Eastern Sea turn to mulberry fields many times. As one proceeds across to Peng Lai, the water comes only up to one's waist. I wonder whether it will turn to dry land once again."

Wang answered:

"The sages say that the Eastern Sea will once again become blowing dust."

Ma Gu wanted to meet Cai Jing's mother, wife, and other (female) members of the family. Now, at this time, Cai's younger brother's wife had given birth to a child only a few days earlier. As soon as Ma Gu saw the young woman, she said:

"Wait! Stop there for a moment and don't come any closer!"

Then she asked that a small amount of uncooked rice be brought to Her. When She got the rice, She threw it on the floor, saying that She did so in order to dispel the unclean influences. When everyone looked down, the rice grains had all changed to pearls.

Wang Yuan then announced to Cai Jing's family:

"I wish to present you all with a gift of fine liquor. This liquor has just been produced by the celestial kitchens. Its flavour is quite strong, so it is unfit for drinking by ordinary people; in fact, in some cases it has been known to burn the intestines. You should mix it with water, and you should not regard this as inappropriate."

With that he added a *dou* of water to a *sheng* of liquor, stirred it, and presented it to the members of Cai Jing's family. On drinking little more than a *sheng* of it each, they were all intoxicated. After a little while, the liquor was all gone. Wang dispatched attendants, saying:

"There's not enough. Go get some more."

Instructing them to buy liquor from a certain old woman in Yuhang. In a short while, the attendants returned saying:

"We have secured one oilcloth bags worth, about five *dou* of liquor."

They also relayed a message from the old woman in Yuhang:

"I fear that this earthly liquor is not fit to be drunk by such eminences."

Ma Gu's fingernails were very long, like those of a bird, and when Cai Jing noticed them, he thought to himself, "My back itches. Wouldn't it be great if I could get Her to scratch my back with those nails?"

Now, Wang Yuan knew what Cai was saying in his heart, so he ordered him bound and whipped, chiding:

"Princess Ma Gu is a divine personage. How dare you think that Her nails could scratch your back!"

A whip began lashing Cai's back with no one seen wielding it. Wang said:

"My whippings are not given without cause."

Shortly after this Wang Yuan and Ma Gu departed, the large quantity of food and drink that Cai Jing's family had prepared were all consumed, even though no one had been seen eating or drinking them. Cai's parents discreetly asked him:

"What sort of divine personage is Lord Wang? At what places does He reside?"

Cai answered:

"He usually resides in Mount Kunlun, but He also travels back and forth to Mount Luofou and Mount Guacang. Atop each of these mountains is a palace from which Lord Wang oversees the affairs of the Celestial Courts. Everyday He is in touch with Heaven above a dozen or more times; in all matters of birth and death on earth, in (the several jurisdictions of) the Five Marchmounts, reports are made first to Lord Wang. When Lord Wang goes forth (from one of the palaces), he sometimes does not take his entire retinue of officials but only rides a yellow donkey and takes about a dozen attendants. Wherever He goes, maintaining an altitude of several thousand feet, the mountains and forests can be seen below; and at each place he arrives, the gods of mountains and waters come forth to greet, welcome, and do obeisance to Him."

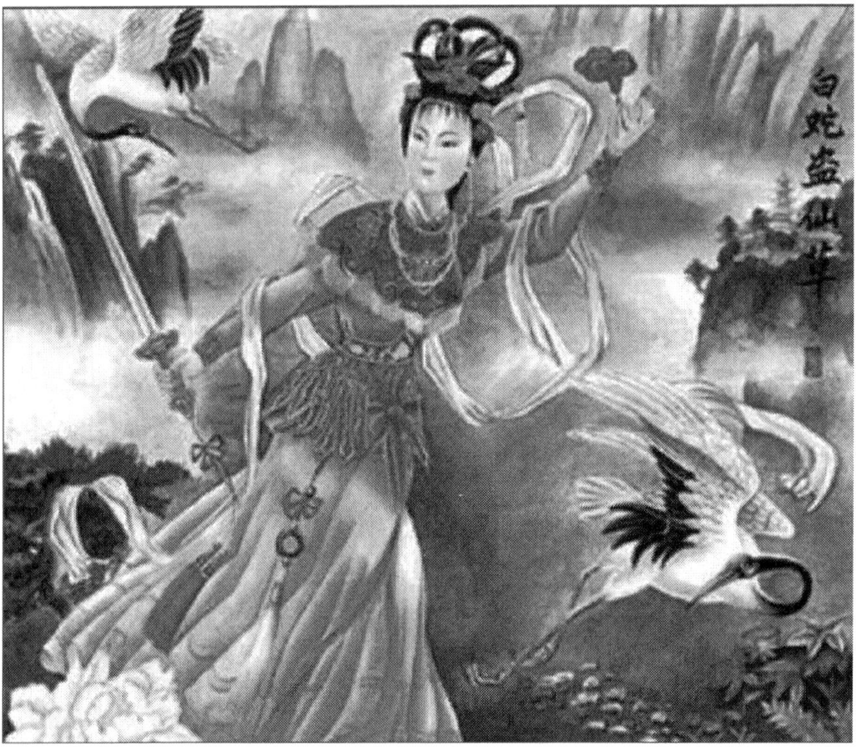
白蛇盗仙草

Traditional Oral Teachings:

The following is a small collection of traditional oral teachings passed down from one devotee to another:

Ma Gu, The Liberator

Ma Gu personifies the goodness in all of humankind.
She freed the slaves from under her evil father.

Traditional Oral Teaching

Cannabis can be used in combination with Ginseng to set forward time in order to reveal future events.

Traditional Oral Teaching

It is recommended to add Cannabis to incense burners in order to achieve immortality.

Traditional Oral Teaching

Accept the offering,
Know the Self.

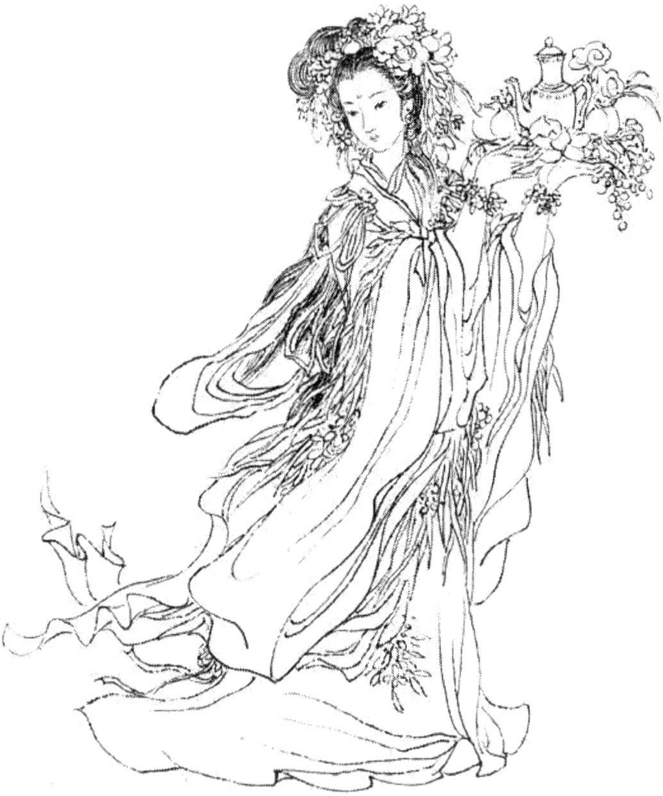

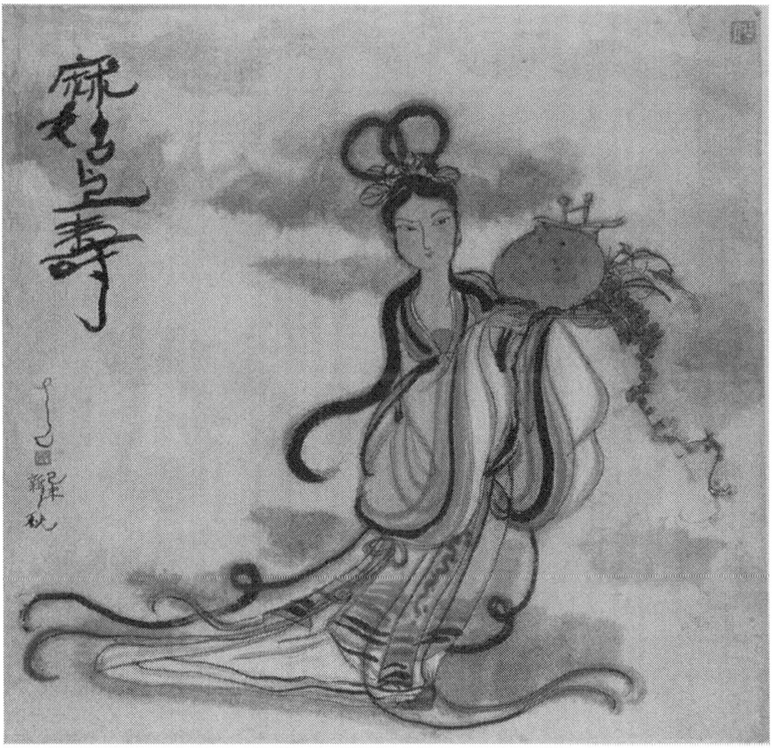
麻姑上壽

Puja and Cannabis Meditation

Devotees to Her Holiness do not follow any written or strict practices when it comes to puja or meditation. Followers are instead encouraged to simply use Cannabis as they feel drawn to and to allow Her Holiness to guide them directly.

That being said here are some guidelines.

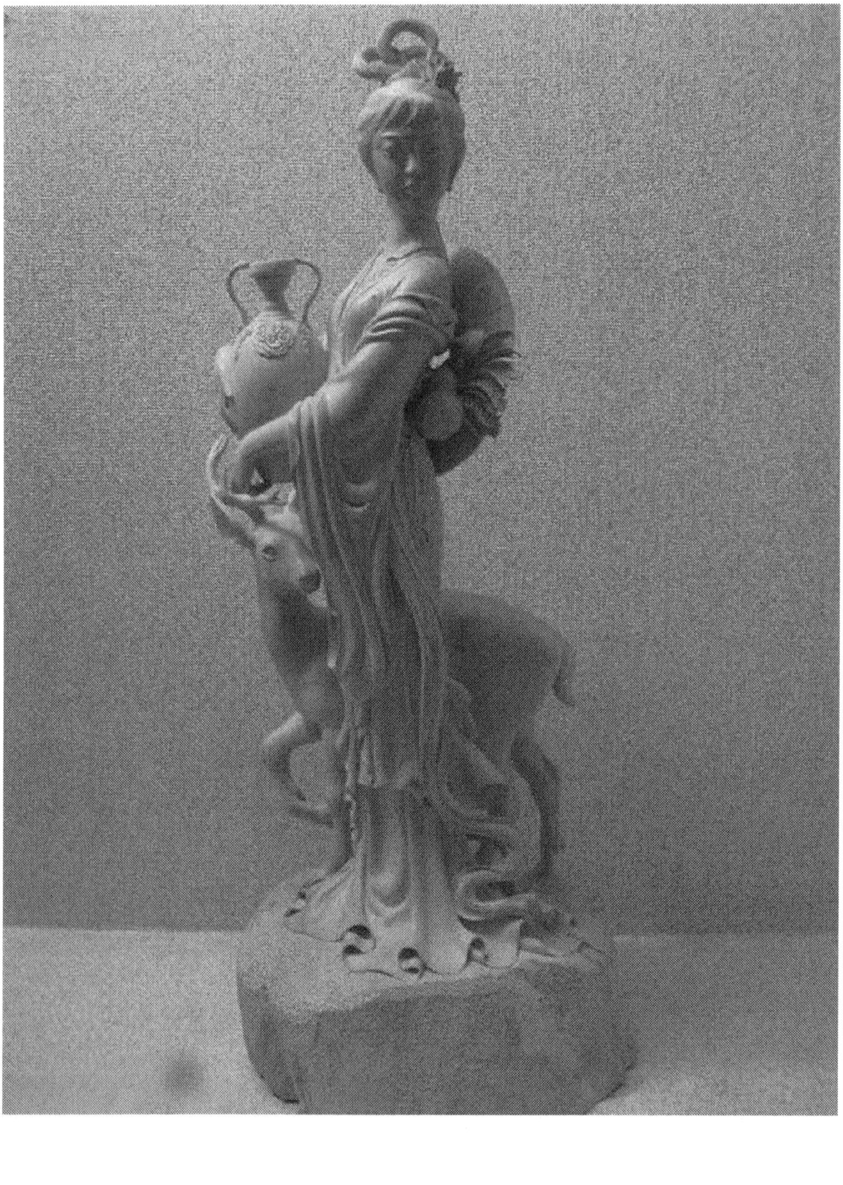

Puja

What is Puja

Puja (poo-jah) is the act of showing reverence to a god, a spirit, or another aspect of the divine through invocations, prayers, songs, and rituals. An essential part of puja for the devotee is making a spiritual connection with the divine. Most often that contact is facilitated through an object: an element of nature, a sculpture, a vessel, a painting, or a print.

During puja an image or other symbol of the god serves as a means of gaining access to the divine. This icon is not the deity itself; rather, it is believed to be filled with the deity's cosmic energy (in our case Her Holiness Princess Ma Gu, Goddess of Cannabis). It is a focal point for honoring and communicating with the god. For the devotee, the icon's artistic merit is important, but is secondary to its spiritual content. The objects are created as receptacles for spiritual energy that allow the devotee to experience direct communication with his or her god.

Choose a Space

The first thing you need to do is to select a space. It may be in your house, where you work, the garden, or wherever you wish, depending on your particular objectives. The important thing is that once you pick a space vigilantly maintain its special, sacred character.

If you want to be traditionally Taoist, you should pick a north wall (so that your altar faces south), and your sacred space should not share a wall with a bathroom, a garage, or any other obvious negative influence. Sun and fresh air will add to the potency of your space.

Building an Altar

Most Taoist Altars and Shrines usually have the following; an incense burner and either an image or representation of a deity, in our case Her Holiness. All other additions for example candles, an offering plate/bowl, flowers etc. are down to the individual (or temple). As long as you follow your heart when creating your Altar or Shrine, I'm sure you will create a very respectful environment for Her Holiness.

How to Bow

Bowing is an integral part of Taoist practice. Taoists are extremely humble before their deities and before the Tao, and they exhibit this humility through frequent ritual bowing. There are countless specific methods of Taoist bowing, but lets only concern ourselves with one very basic form.

Face your altar. Stand with your feet together but not touching. Your body should be like it is standing at attention (strong but flexible) and your spine should be straight from the crown of your head to the base of your tailbone. Start with your hands at your sides, and as you slowly raise your hands place your left palm over your right fist (this is the union of Yin and Yang - Earth and Heaven - Scholar and Warrior - The marriage of Yin and Yang). You should raise your hands to a level somewhere between chest (heart) and eye level (upper dantian). As your hands reach their destination, execute a short bow from your waist. Your eyes should face down and your head should go lower than your image /

representation of Her Holiness. This is to show respect and trust.

How to Make Offerings

Taoist altar offerings can be quite complicated affairs, and may consist of fruit, grain, various herbs, water, and rice wine. Although devotees may offer these to Ma Gu during festivals and holidays it is not necessary within the Way Of Infinite Harmony tradition to do so.

To start any offering to Her Holiness you must first bow and offer Her Holiness some Cannabis, whether this be in the form of you smoking or eating it, or burning some in an incense burner. Once you have have done this devotees believe you have opened a door to heaven and should therefore be very respectful in your manners and language. You may now begin to meditate and/or pray.

Once you are finished, bow and thank the Ma Gu for listening to your prayers, helping you with meditation, and accepting your offerings.

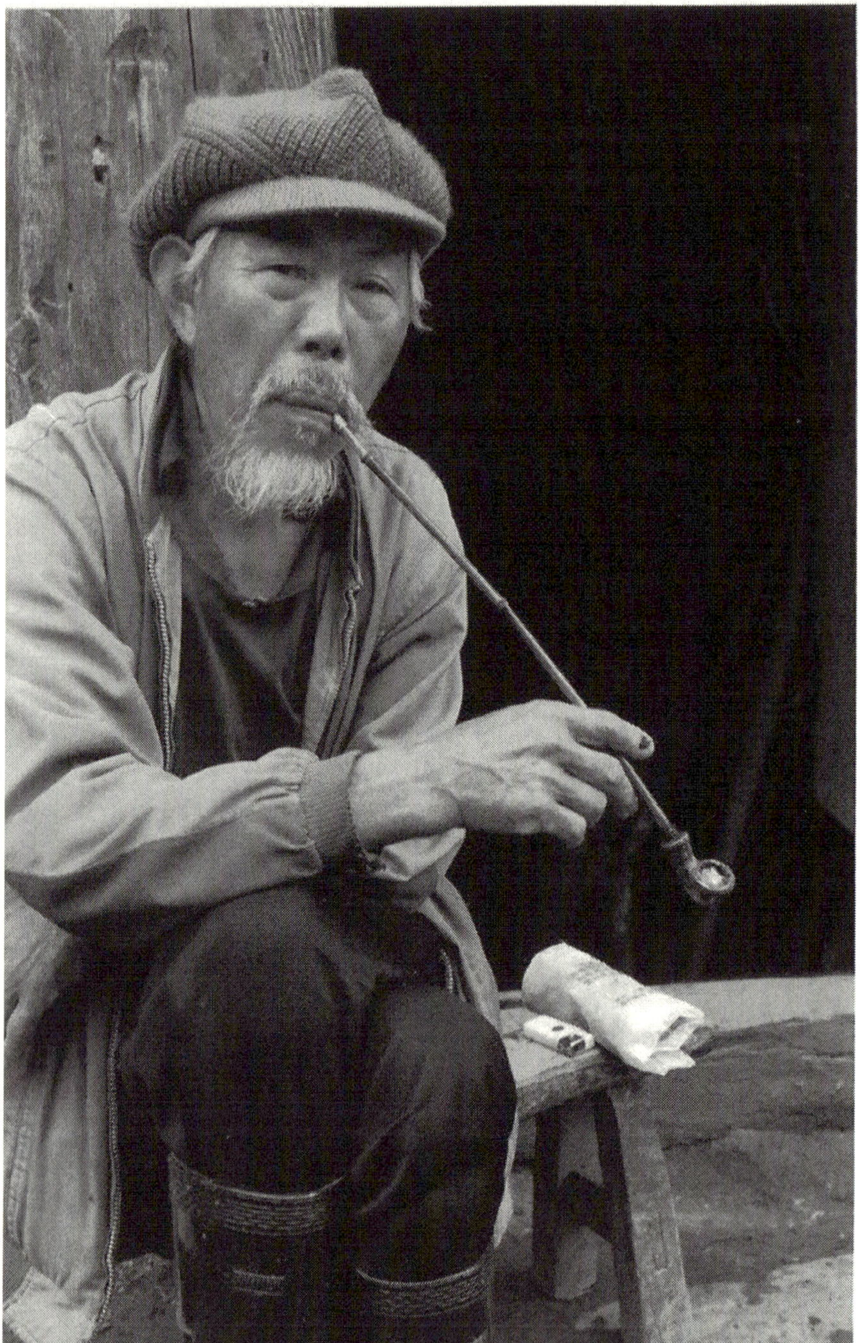

Meditation

As already stated there are no strict guidelines for devotees to follow with regard to meditation in the Way Of Infinite Harmony. Devotees instead believe being under the influence of Cannabis (and therefore in the embrace of Her Holiness) is in itself an enlightening and meditative state.

Devotee's point to a number of different examples of how Cannabis use itself is meditative:

> Cannabis improves our ability to focus the mind toward investigation of Awareness (of human consciousness).
>
> Cannabis encourages us to become more Self-aware. (Increased Self-knowledge is a major component of spiritual development within the Way Of Infinite Harmony tradition.)
>
> Cannabis causes us to be more present in the moment thus revealing a less delusional interpretation of reality.
>
> Cannabis shows us that learned social rules can become unconsciously ingrained.
>
> Cannabis allows insights into others. This deeper perception offers an opportunity to evaluate human behavior at a comfortable arms length.
>
> Cannabis not only amplifies thoughts and feelings, but it also moves them in a happier, more euphoric direction. The process of Immortalization (Enlightenment) and seeing the unquestioned prejudices of our everyday walking around self can come as a shock. Cannabis makes us feel good and the heavy dose of reality is easier to accept when happy.

Cannabis reduces our natural tendency toward feeling in control. As we develop spiritually one realization is that we were never in control. Cannabis makes this realization easier to see and accept. As we become more open to genuine experience, it becomes easier to ask the tough questions that lead toward heightened Self-knowledge.

Cannabis creates a sense of wonderment that encourages us to ponder the nature of the subconscious and how much of our actions are deliberate.

As we grow in awareness through Cannabis, the interdependent relationship of humanity and the biosphere becomes increasingly clear.

Cannabis amplifies emotions. As these emotions become amplified, they are easier to recognize and evaluate (fearlessly) at an arm's length. When we can become aware of emotions, we have an opportunity to recognize that our mind has drawn a line across the entire field of experience and everything inside that line is "me" and everything outside that line is "not me". Understanding our maps of human consciousness and waking up to how the "Self" is defined, begins with a recognition of our interior versus exterior dichotomy.

What to Expect

As you become more experienced using Cannabis spiritually, you will experience benefits of many types, including improvements in your energy flow, better overall health, and most importantly, your connection to the Tao and Ma Gu will dramatically increase.

Pilgrimage & Festivals

The search for Ma Gu Shan (Ma Gu Mountain) is both the inner search for the Tao (Self / All-That-Is) and the act of pilgrimage to sites considered holy by devotees.

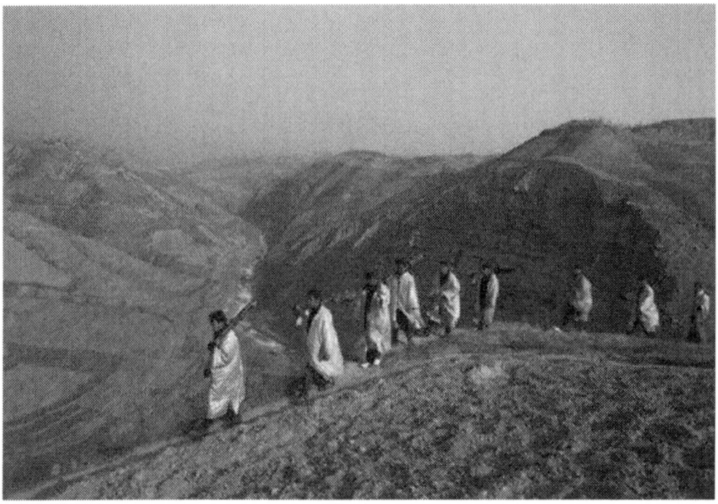

Ma Gu Temple

The primary pilgrimage site, and only known temple solely dedicated to Her Holiness that has survived the Cultural Revolution in China, is Ma Gu Temple in Yue Gu Temple complex, Yantai, Shangdong Province, China. This is the place where Ma Gu practiced and attained Immortality and the entire complex is considered the spiritual home of The Way Of Infinite Harmony.

Ma Gu Temple

Ma Gu Wonderland

The second most important pilgrimage site is "Ma Gu Wonderland". Situated at the base of Mount Heng in Hunan Province, Ma Gu Wonderland is the site of Ma Gu's Pond (the pool mentioned in "Ma Gu, The Princess of Cannabis Her Generation and Mission") which locals say Ma Gu visits on the third day of the third month in the Chinese lunar calendar, in the centre of which stands a beautiful statue of Her Holiness. Also here is Ma Gu Waterfall (considered one of the most scenic in China).

Ma Gu Pond

The Ma Gu Mountains

Well known to all Taoists are the "Ma Gu Mountains" the primary one being Ma Gu Shan (麻姑山 "Ma Gu Mountain") which is located in Nancheng. Taoists regard its Danxia Dong (丹霞洞 "Cinnabar Cloud Grotto") as the 28th of 36 sacred *dongtian* (洞天 "Grotto-heavens / heaven-reaching grottos"). A number of shrines and caves devoted to Her Holiness cover the mountain.

Entrance to Ma Gu Shan

A second Ma Gu Mountain is located in Jianchang county (建昌, near Nanfeng, 南豐).

Ma Gu Waterfall

Festivals & Important Dates

There are historically 3 dates in the tradition that are considered particularly important.

The primary one is Ma Gu's birthday on the 6th day of the 6th lunar month. This day is entirely set aside by devotees to give praise and thanks for Her Creation.

The second is the traditional date for harvesting Hemp in ancient China, the 7th day of the 7th lunar month, and is the day for the "Fire Ritual" as described in "When The World Was Green" with devotees burning large amounts of Cannabis in Her honor.

Third is the date that Ma Gu is said to appear at Ma Gu Pond and the date of the Queen Mother of The West's Peach Banquet, the 3rd day of the 3rd lunar month, with a sea of pilgrims going to the site to catch a glimpse of Her Holiness.

The Fire Ritual

献寿图

www.WayOfInfiniteHarmony.org

Appendix

Different Accounts

The following are synopses of texts that are not Way Of Infinite Harmony teachings and are seen as different accounts written by other sects.

(These non-sect teachings are included so that the book you hold in your hands contains ALL the teachings that have ever been written about Her Holiness.)

Arrayed Marvels

This was a late second or early third century collection of alternate accounts attributed to Cao Pi. In it is a version of the incident of Cai Jing's inappropriate fantasy concerning Ma Gu and Her luxuriant four-inch nails. Here, Cai Jing's home is located in Dongyang: he is not whipped but rather flung to the ground, his eyes running blood: and Ma Gu Herself is the one who reads his thoughts and does the punishment.

Garden of Marvels

This is from another collection of alternate accounts. Written by Liu Jingshu in the early fifth century.

In it the Cult of Ma Gu is described as that of a powerful but wronged human being, rooted to a particular locality, in an attempt to portray Ma Gu as a "ghost" rather than an Immortal.

"During Qin times there was a Temple to Maid Ma beside a lake. When alive, She had possessed the arts of the Tao. She could walk on water in Her shoes. Later, She violated the laws of the Tao, and Her father, out of anger, murdered Her and dumped Her body in the lake. Following the current, it floated on the waves until it reached the (present site of) the temple. A subordinate shaman directed that She be en-coffined but not immediately buried. Very soon a square, lacquered coffin appeared in the shrine hall. (From then on,) at the end and beginning of each lunar month, people there could make out through the fog an indistinct figure, wearing shoes. Fishing and hunting were prohibited in the area of the temple, and violators would always become lost or drown. Shamans said that it was because the Maid had suffered a painful death and hated to see other beings cruelly killed."

Commoner of Fuyang

This is from another (un-named) collection of alternate accounts, roughly contemporaneous with "Garden of Marvels". In it Ma Gu is referred to as "commoner of Fuyang" and no mention is made of Her divinity or transcendence.

Having caught a creature with features of both sea turtle and serpent, She and Her companion, one Hua Ben, prepare it (after its complete transformation into a turtle) and eat it. She soon grows ill, and something blocks Her throat; when She opens Her mouth toward Hua Ben, he is terrified to see a snake opening its mouth and flicking its tongue toward him from inside Maid Ma's throat. Later, when Maid Ma catches sight of the stripped skin of a snake that has been inside Hua's home and prepared as a meal (a sample of which Ma Gu has already eaten and found delicious), she vomits blood and dies.